The
Nature
and Mission
of the
Church

The Nature and Mission of the Church

A Stage on the Way to a Common Statement

Faith and Order Paper 198

World Council of Churches, Geneva

Cover design: Rob Lucas

ISBN 2-8254-1463-8

Printed in France

Table of Contents

Introduction

1. Since its beginning, and especially at the First World Conference, Lausanne, Switzerland, 1927, the Faith and Order Movement identified the unity of the Church as the very reason for its existence. Thus the By-Laws of the Faith and Order Commission state that its aim is:

> to proclaim the oneness of the Church of Jesus Christ and to call the churches to the goal of visible unity in one faith and one Eucharistic fellowship, expressed in worship and in common life in Christ, in order that the world may believe.[1]

Since Amsterdam, 1948, this goal has been at the heart of the World Council of Churches itself. Moreover, in the Assemblies of the World Council of Churches, the particular contribution of Faith and Order has been to deepen a common understanding of this goal and of the ways to realise it. A significant contribution has been made from the Canberra Assembly (1991) in the statement "The Church as Koinonia: Gift and Calling".[2] This statement claims that koinonia is both the foundation and the way of living a life together in visible unity. This was echoed in the theme of the Fifth World Conference on Faith and Order, Towards Koinonia in Faith, Life and Witness. The process on "Towards a Common Understanding and Vision of the World Council of Churches"[3] again underlines the common calling of the churches as the search for visible unity.

2. All the major documents issued by Faith and Order contribute in some way or other to the understanding of the nature and mission of the Church. Moreover, *Baptism, Eucharist and Ministry*,[4] *Confessing the One Faith: An Ecumenical Explication of the Apostolic Faith as it is Confessed in the Nicene-Constantinopolitan Creed (381)*,[5] and *Church and World: the Unity of the*

Church and the Renewal of Human Community,[6] sent to the churches for response and reception, are ways of keeping alive in the churches the imperative of Christ's call to visible unity and the essential characteristics of that unity. The recent studies of Faith and Order such as on Baptism, Ethnic Identity, Anthropology and Hermeneutics have a continuing relevance to the subject. Also, the absolute centrality of ecclesiology to the ecumenical movement has been recently reaffirmed by the Special Commission on the participation of the Orthodox churches in the WCC. In the last decade work on ecclesiology and ethics (which continued the studies, for example, on racism and the community of women and men in the Church) has contributed to the understanding of our common Christian calling in the service of humanity and creation. In its turn Faith and Order continually receives insights about the unity to which God calls us from responses of the churches to its studies, the results of the bilateral dialogues, the work in other areas of the World Council of Churches and from reflection on the experience of the United and Uniting Churches.

A. This Study

3. A study on the nature and purpose of the Church was strongly recommended by the Fifth World Conference on Faith and Order in Santiago de Compostela, Spain (1993). In endorsing this study the Standing Commission of Faith and Order identified the following reasons why this call is particularly timely:

- the time is right for Faith and Order to reflect on the different insights which its own studies offer to an understanding of the nature and mission of the Church;

- the opportunity is there for Faith and Order to draw upon the fruits of the work of other areas of the WCC and of the bilateral theological agreements;
- growth in fellowship is being experienced between Christians at local, national and world levels, not least of all in the experience of united and uniting churches;
- particular challenges in many regions call out for Christians to address together what it means to be the Church in that place;
- the situation of the world demands and deserves a credible witness to unity in diversity which is God's gift for the whole of humanity.
- the experience of the BEM process and an increasing interest in ecclesiology in many churches provide fresh insights into how many Christians understand being the Church;
- political changes and challenges in recent years are significantly altering the context in which many churches exist and therefore how they seek to understand themselves.

4. The quest for visible unity of the churches is not pursued in a vacuum but by particular Christian communities in specific and varied situations. For this reason, no single text can say everything there is to say about the Church. Faith and Order invites churches in different parts of the world to enrich this study with appropriate regional material to enable their own congregations and church members to engage directly with themes which are necessarily expressed here in quite general terms. The Commission especially encourages reflection based on actual stories of Christian life and witness in different parts of the world so that both the particular and the universal features of the Church can be more clearly understood.

This is important above all from the perspective of mission, which is one of guiding themes of this study. Mission is not an abstraction but is lived in response to the grace of God as God sends his Church in faithful witness in the actual situations of each society. While human need is universal, the forms which that need takes vary. For some the struggle with HIV/AIDS is paramount, for others finding a language to express spiritual reality in apparently materialistic cultures. For some war, poverty and injustice are the main context for mission, for others relations with other faiths. For some the issue is spiritual and for others material want. For these reasons this text attempts to be alert to the diversity of contexts; at the same time it seeks to offer the churches some common ecclesiological perspectives which might encourage practical local reflection and so serve the quest for Christian unity in diverse environments.

B. Purpose and Method

5. The purpose of this study is finally to give expression to what the churches can now say together about the nature and mission of the Church and, within that agreement, to explore the extent to which the remaining church-dividing issues may be overcome. Thus, in the precedent Baptism, Eucharist and Ministry the process seems to evolve into what could be called a "convergence" text. The present text is to enable churches to begin the first steps towards the recognition of a convergence that has emerged in a multilateral context.

6. The **main text** represents common perspectives which can be claimed, largely as a result of the work of the bilateral and multilateral discussions of the past fifty years and of the changed relationships between the churches in this period. **The material inside the**

boxes explores areas where differences remain both within and between churches. Some of these differences may come to be seen by some as expressions of legitimate diversity, by others as church-dividing. While the main text invites the churches to discover, or rediscover, how much they in fact have in common in their understanding of the Church, the text in the boxes offers the opportunity for churches to reflect on the extent to which their divergences are church-dividing. In the perspective of growing convergences, the hope is that churches will be helped to recognise in one another the Church of Jesus Christ and be encouraged to take steps on the way towards visible unity.

7. The Faith and Order Commission invited churches, commissions, theological institutes, ecumenical councils and individuals to reflect on the text *The Nature and Purpose of the Church: A Stage on the Way to a Common Statement.*[7] Faith and Order is grateful to those who responded to this invitation but is conscious that the responses were not fully representative of all the churches. Nevertheless, we hope that the changes occasioned by the suggestions will be evident. One of the frequent suggestions was to strengthen the text's emphasis on mission. In making this change both in title and in content we have tried to ensure that these changes confirm the continuity with the previous work, but also to meet the new concerns.

C. The Invitation

8. In God's providence the Church exists, not for itself alone, but to serve in God's work of reconciliation and for the praise and glory of God. The self-understanding of the church is essential for its proper response to its vocation. Despite diversities of language and theology, mutual understanding can grow when people are willing to allow each other space to

use their own language to describe themselves. For example, to participate in a council of churches does not imply that all members regard all other members as churches in the same sense in which they regard themselves. Such courtesy is not merely pragmatic, but can contribute to a spiritual encounter between different communities in which as trust grows it becomes possible to face the theological issues together. Hence the crucial importance of this study on the nature and the mission of the Church.

In the light of this new revised text we request especially the churches to respond, in the manner they deem most appropriate, to the following questions:

- *Does this study document correctly identify our common ecclesiological convictions, as well as the issues which continue to divide us?*
- *Does this study document reflect an emerging convergence on the nature and mission of the Church?*
- *Are there significant matters in which the concerns of your church are not adequately addressed?*
- *Insofar as this study document provides a helpful framework for further ecclesiological discussions among the churches:*
  - *How can this study document help your church, together with others, take concrete steps towards unity?*
  - *What suggestions would you make for the future development of this text?*

I. The Church of the Triune God

A. The Nature of the Church

(I) THE CHURCH AS A GIFT OF GOD: CREATION OF THE WORD AND OF THE HOLY SPIRIT (CREATURA VERBI ET CREATURA SPIRITUS)

9. The Church is called into being by the Father "who so loved the world that he gave his only begotten Son, that whoever believes in him shall not perish, but have eternal life" (Jn 3:16) and who sent the Holy Spirit to lead these believers into all truth, reminding them of all that Jesus taught (cf. Jn 14:26). The Church is thus the creature of God's Word and of the Holy Spirit. It belongs to God, is God's gift and cannot exist by and for itself. Of its very nature it is missionary, called and sent to serve, as an instrument of the Word and the Spirit, as a witness to the Kingdom of God.

10. The Church is centred and grounded in the Word of God. This Word has become manifest in history in various ways. "… it is the Word of God made flesh: Jesus Christ, incarnate, crucified and risen. Then it is the word as spoken in God's history with God's people and recorded in the scriptures of the Old and New Testaments as a testimony to Jesus Christ. Third, it is the word as heard and proclaimed in the preaching, witness and action of the Church."[8] The Church is the communion of those who, by means of their encounter with the Word, stand in a living relationship with God, who speaks to them and calls forth their trustful response; it is the communion of the faithful. This is the common vocation of every Christian and is exemplified by the faithful responsiveness of Mary to the angel of the annunciation: "Here I am, the servant of the Lord; let it be with me according to your word" (Lk 1:38). For this reason Mary has often been seen as a symbol of the Church and of the individual Christian, called to be Jesus' "brother and sister and mother" in doing the will of his Father in heaven (cf. Mt

14

12:50). Thus the Church is the creature of God's Word
(creatura Verbi), the Gospel, which, as a living voice, creates and nourishes the Church throughout the ages. This
divine Word is witnessed to and heard through Scripture.
Incarnate in Jesus Christ, the Word is testified to by the
Church and proclaimed in preaching, in Sacraments, and
in service (cf. Mt 28:19-20; Lk 1:2; Acts 1:8; 1Cor 15:1-11).

11. Faith called forth by the Word of God is brought
about by the action of the Holy Spirit (cf. 1 Cor 12:3).
According to the Scripture, the Word and the Spirit are
inseparable. As the communion of the faithful, the
Church therefore is also the creature of the Holy Spirit
(Creatura Spiritus). Just as in the life of Christ the Holy
Spirit was active from the very conception of Jesus
through the paschal mystery and remains even now the
Spirit of the risen Lord, so also in the life of the Church
the Spirit forms Christ in believers and in their community. The Spirit incorporates human beings into the body of
Christ through faith and baptism, enlivens and strength-
ens them as the body of Christ nourished and sustained
in the Lord's Supper, and leads them to the full accom-
plishment of their vocation.

12. Being the creature of God's own Word and Spirit,
the Church is one, holy, catholic and apostolic. These
essential attributes flow from and illustrate the Church's
dependence upon God. The Church is one because God is
the one creator and redeemer (cf. Jn 17:11, Eph 4:1-6), who
binds the Church to himself by Word and Spirit and
makes it a foretaste and instrument for the redemption of
all created reality. The Church is holy because God is the
holy one (cf. Is 6:3; Lev 11:44-45) who sent his Son Jesus
Christ to overcome all unholiness and to call human
beings to become merciful like his Father (cf. Lk 6:36),
sanctifying the Church by his word of forgiveness in the
Holy Spirit and making it his own, the body of Christ
(Eph 5:26-27). The Church is catholic because God is the

fullness of life "who desires everyone to be saved and to come to the knowledge of the truth" (1 Tim 2:4), and who, through Word and Spirit, makes his people the place and instrument of his saving and life-giving presence, the community "in which, in all ages, the Holy Spirit makes the believers participants in Christ's life and salvation, regardless of their sex, race or social position".[9] It is apostolic because the Word of God, sent by the Father, creates and sustains the Church. This word of God is made known to us through the Gospel primarily and normatively borne witness to by the apostles (cf. Eph 2:20; Rev 21:14), making the communion of the faithful a community that lives in, and is responsible for, the succession of the apostolic truth expressed in faith and life throughout the ages.

13. The Church is not merely the sum of individual believers in communion with God, nor primarily the mutual communion of individual believers among themselves. It is their common partaking in the life of God (2 Pet 1:4), who as Trinity, is the source and focus of all communion. Thus the Church is both a divine and a human reality.

The Institutional Dimension of the Church and the Work of the Holy Spirit

All churches agree that God creates the Church and binds it to himself through the Holy Spirit by means of the living voice of the Gospel proclaimed in preaching and in the Sacraments. Yet they have different convictions as to:

(a) whether the preaching and the Sacraments are the means of, or simply witnesses to, the activity of the Spirit through the divine Word, which comes about in an immediate internal action upon the hearts of the believers;

(b) the institutional implications and presuppositions of the Church's being Creatura Verbi: for some the ordained ministry, particularly episcopacy, is the effective means, for some a guarantee of the presence of truth and power of the Word and Spirit of God in the Church; for others the fact that the ordained ministry, as well as the witness of all believers, are subject to error and sin excludes such a judgement, the power and reliability of God's truth being grounded in the sovereignty of his Word and Spirit which works through – but if necessary also counter to – the given institutional structures of the Church;

(c) The theological importance of institutional continuity, particularly continuity in episcopacy: whereas for some churches such institutional continuity is the necessary means and guarantee of the Church's continuity in apostolic faith, for others continuity in apostolic faith is, under certain circumstances, being kept in spite of – and even through – the break of institutional continuity.

It remains for future theological work to find out whether these differences are real disagreements or mere differences in emphasis that can be reconciled with each other.

(II) BIBLICAL INSIGHTS

14. The Almighty God, who calls the Church into being and unites it to himself through his Word and the Holy Spirit, is the Triune God, Father, Son and Holy Spirit. The Church is related to each of these divine "Persons" in a particular way. These relations shed light upon different dimensions of the Church's life.

15. Many insights pertinent to the nature and mission of the Church are present in Scripture although it does

not offer a systematic ecclesiology. The biblical understanding governing the present text is based on the common conviction that Scripture is normative and therefore provides a uniquely privileged source for understanding the nature and mission of the Church. Subsequent reflection must always engage and be consonant with the biblical teaching. The interplay of different kinds of material – accounts of the faith of the early communities, evidence regarding their worship and practice of discipleship, indications of the various roles of service and leadership and, finally, images and metaphors used to express the nature of the community – all provide resources for the development of a biblical understanding of the Church. There also exists a rich resource to be explored in the interpretation of Scripture over the course of history. The same Holy Spirit who inspired the earliest communities guides the followers of Jesus in each time and each place as they strive to be faithful to the Gospel. This is what is understood by the living tradition of the Church.

16. It is essential to acknowledge the wide diversity of insights into the nature and mission of the Church which can be found in the various books of the New Testament and in their interpretation in later history. Diversity appears not as accidental to the life of the Christian community, but as an aspect of its catholicity, a quality that reflects the fact that it is part of the Father's design that the story of salvation in Christ be incarnational. Thus, diversity is a gift of God to the Church.[10] Not only do various passages of the New Testament use the plural "churches" to denote that there are a variety of local churches (cf. Acts 15:41; Rom 16:16; 1 Cor 4:17; 7:17; 11:16; 16:1, 19; 2 Cor 8:1; Gal 1:2; 1 Thess 2:14), without thereby contradicting the conviction that Christ's body is one (Eph 4:4), but also one finds variety among the ecclesiological themes and insights addressed by individual books. The inclusion of such plurality within the one

canon of the New Testament testifies to the compatibility of unity and diversity. Indeed, the discussion of the one body with many members (cf. 1 Cor 12-14) suggests that unity is possible only through the proper co-ordination of the diverse gifts of the Triune God.

17. To honour the varied biblical insights into the nature and mission of the church, various approaches are required. Four – "people of God", "Body of Christ", "Temple of the Holy Spirit" and koinonia – have been chosen for particular comment because, taken together, they illuminate the New Testament vision of the Church in relation to the Triune God. A fully rounded approach to the mystery of the Church requires the use and interaction of all biblical images and insights (in addition to those mentioned, "vine", "flock", "bride", "household" and "covenant community"), each of which contributes something vital to our understanding. These images counterbalance each other and compensate each others' limitations. Since every image comes out of a particular cultural context they suggest both insufficiencies and possibilities. This text seeks to relate to Scripture as a whole, not playing off one passage against another, but trying always to honour the totality of the Biblical witness.

(a) The Church as People of God
18. In the call of Abraham, God was choosing for himself a holy people. The recalling of this election and vocation found frequent expression in the words of the prophets: "I will be their God and they shall be my people" (Jer 31:33; Ez 37:27; echoed in 2 Cor 6:16; Heb 8:10). Through the Word (dabhar) and the Spirit (rû'ah), God fashioned one from among the nations as servant for the salvation of all (cf. Is 49:1-6). The election of Israel marked a decisive moment in the unfolding realisation of the plan of salvation. The covenant between God and his people

entailed many things for example, the Torah, the land and common worship, including the call to act with justice and to speak the truth. At the same time, the covenant was also clearly a relationship of communion (cf. Hos. 2; Ez. 16). But it is also a gracious gift, a dynamic impulse to communion which is evident throughout the history of the people of Israel, even when the community breaks the covenant. In the light of the ministry, teaching, death and resurrection of Jesus and the sending of the Holy Spirit at Pentecost, the Christian community believes that God sent his Son to bring the possibility of communion for each person with others and with God, thus manifesting the gift of God for the whole world. There is a genuine newness in the covenant initiated by Christ. Nevertheless, as "the Israel of God" (Gal 6:16), the Church remains related, in a mysterious way, to the Jewish people, even as a branch is grafted onto the rich root of an olive tree (cf. Rom 11:11-36).

19. In the Old Testament, the people of Israel is a pilgrim people journeying towards the fulfilment of the promise that in Abraham all the nations of the earth shall be blessed. In Christ this promise is fulfilled when, on the cross, the dividing wall between Jew and Gentile is broken down (cf. Eph 2:14). The Church, embracing both Jew and Gentile, is a "chosen race, a royal priesthood, a holy nation", "God's own people" (1 Peter 2:9-10), a community of prophets. While acknowledging the unique priesthood of Jesus Christ, whose one sacrifice institutes the new covenant (cf. Heb 9:15), Christians are called to express by their lives the fact that they have been named a "royal priesthood" and "holy nation". In Christ who offered himself, Christians offer their whole being "as a living sacrifice, holy and acceptable to God, which is your spiritual worship" (Rom 12:1). Every member participates in the priesthood of the whole Church. No one exercises that priesthood apart from the unique priesthood of

Christ, nor in isolation from the other members of the body. As a prophetic and royal people, Christians seek to witness to the will of God and to influence the course of events of the world. Throughout the ages, the Church of God continues the way of pilgrimage to the eternal rest prepared for it (cf. Heb 4:9-11). It is a prophetic sign of the fulfilment God will bring about through Christ by the power of the Spirit.

(b) The Church as the Body of Christ

20. According to the design of God, those "who once were far off have become near by the blood of Christ. For he is our peace" (Eph 2:13-14). He overcame the enmity between Jew and Gentile, reconciling both with God in one body through the cross (cf. Eph 2:16). This body is the body of Christ, which is the Church (cf. Eph 1:23). Christ is the abiding head of his body and at the same time the one who, by the presence of the Spirit, gives life to it. He who cleanses and sanctifies the body (cf. Eph 5:26) is also the one in whom "we, though many, are one body" (Rom 12:5; cf. 1 Cor 12:12). The image of the body of Christ in the New Testament includes these two dimensions, one expressed in 1 Corinthians and Romans, the other developed in Ephesians.

21. It is through faith and baptism that human beings become members of Christ in the Holy Spirit (cf. 1 Cor 12:3-13). Through the Lord's Supper their participation in this body is renewed again and again (cf. 1 Cor 10:16). It is the same Holy Spirit who confers the manifold gifts to the members of the body (cf. 1 Cor 12:4; 7-11) and brings forth their unity (cf. 1 Cor 12:12). All members of Christ are given gifts for the building up of the body (cf. Rom 12:4-8; 1 Cor 12:4-30). The diversity and specific nature of these gifts enrich the Church's life and enable a better response to its vocation to be servant of the Lord and effective sign used by God for furthering the Kingdom in

the world. Thus the image of "body of Christ", though explicitly and primarily referring to the Christological dimension of the Church, at the same time has deep pneumatological implications.

(c) The Church as Temple of the Holy Spirit

22. Reference to the constitutive relationship between Church and Holy Spirit runs through the whole New Testament witness. While there is no explicit image for this relationship, a vivid example is the account of the descent of tongues of fire upon the disciples gathered in the upper room on the morning of Pentecost (cf. Acts 2:1-4). The New Testament imagery that most closely approximates to this relationship is that of "temple" and "house". This is so because the relationship of the Spirit to the Church is one of indwelling, of giving life from within. The Holy Spirit so enlivens the community that it becomes a herald of, and an instrument for, that general transformation of the whole cosmos for which all creation groans (cf. Rom. 8:22-23), the new heavens and new earth (cf. Rev. 21:1).

23. Built on the foundation of the apostles and prophets the Church is God's household, a holy temple in which the Holy Spirit lives and is active. By the power of the Holy Spirit believers grow into "a holy temple in the Lord" (Eph 2:21-22), into a "spiritual house" (1 Pet 2:5). Filled with the Holy Spirit, they witness (cf. Acts 1:8), pray, love, work and serve in the power of the Spirit, leading a life worthy of their calling, eager to maintain the unity of the Spirit in the bond of peace (cf. Eph 4:1-3).

(d) The Church as Koinonia/Communion

24. The biblical notion of koinonia has become central in the quest for a common understanding of the nature of the Church and its visible unity. The term koinonia (communion, participation, fellowship, sharing) is found not

only in the New Testament but also in later periods, especially in patristic and Reformation writings which describe the Church. Although in some periods the term largely fell out of use, it is being reclaimed today as a key to understanding the nature and mission of the Church. Due to its richness of meaning, it is also ecumenically useful in appreciating the various forms and extent of communion already enjoyed by the Churches.

25. The relationship between God, humanity and the whole of creation is a fundamental theme of Scripture. In the narrative of creation, man and woman are fashioned in God's image, bearing an inherent capacity and longing for communion with God, with one another and with creation as its stewards (cf. Gen 1-2). Thus, the whole of creation has its integrity in koinonia with God. Communion is rooted in the order of creation itself and is realised, in part, in natural relationships of family and kinship, of tribe and people. At the heart of the Old Testament is the special relationship, the covenant, established by God between God and the chosen people (cf. Ex 19:4-6; Hos 2:18-23).

26. God's purpose in creation is distorted by human sin, failure and disobedience to God's will and by rebellion against him (cf. Gen 3-4; Rom 1:18-3:20). Sin damages the relationship between God, human beings and the created order. But God persists in faithfulness despite the sin and error of the people. The dynamic history of God's restoring and increasing koinonia reaches its culmination and fulfilment in the perfect communion of a new heaven and a new earth established by Jesus Christ (cf. Rev 21).

27. The biblical images already treated, as well as others such as "the flock" (Jn 10:16), "the vine" (Is 5; Jn 15), "the bride" of Christ (Rev 21:2; Eph 5:25-32), "God's house" (Heb 3:1-6), "a new covenant" (Heb 8:8-13) and "the holy city, the new Jerusalem" (Rev 21:2), evoke the

nature and quality of the relationship of God's people to God, to one another and to the created order. The term koinonia expresses the reality to which these images refer.

28. The basic verbal form from which the noun koinonia derives means "to have something in common", "to share", "to participate", "to have part in", "to act together" or "to be in a contractual relationship involving obligations of mutual accountability". The word koinonia appears in significant passages, such as the sharing in the Lord's Supper (cf. 1 Cor 10:16), the reconciliation of Paul with Peter, James and John (cf. Gal 2:9), the collection for the poor (cf. Rom 15:26; 2 Cor 8:3-4) and the experience and witness of the Church (cf. Acts 2:42-45).

29. Through the death and resurrection of Christ, by the power of the Holy Spirit, Christians enter into fellowship with God and with one another in the life and love of God: "We declare to you what we have seen and heard so that you also may have fellowship with us; and truly our fellowship is with the Father and with his Son Jesus Christ" (1 Jn 1:3).

30. The Good News is the offer to all people of the free gift of being born into the life of communion with God and thus with one another (cf. 1 Tim 2:4, 2 Pet 2:9). Paul speaks of the relationship of believers (cf. Gal. 2:20) to their Lord as being "in Christ" (2 Cor 5:17) and of Christ being in the believer, through the indwelling of the Holy Spirit.

31. It is only by virtue of God's gift of grace through Jesus Christ that deep, lasting communion is made possible; by faith and baptism, persons participate in the mystery of Christ's death, burial and resurrection (cf. Phil 3:10-11). United to Christ, through the Holy Spirit, they are thus joined to all who are "in Christ": they belong to the communion – the new community of the risen Lord. Because koinonia is a participation in Christ crucified and

risen, it is also part of the mission of the Church to share in the sufferings and hopes of humankind.

32. Visible and tangible signs of the new life of communion are expressed in receiving and sharing the faith of the apostles; breaking and sharing the Eucharistic bread; praying with and for one another and for the needs of the world; serving one another in love; participating in each other's joys and sorrows; giving material aid; proclaiming and witnessing to the good news in mission and working together for justice and peace. The communion of the Church consists not of independent individuals but of persons in community, all of whom contribute to its flourishing.

33. The Church exists for the glory and praise of God, to serve the reconciliation of humankind, in obedience to the command of Christ. It is the will of God that the communion in Christ, which is realised in the Church, should embrace the whole creation (cf. Eph 1:10). The Church, as communion, is instrumental to God's ultimate purpose (cf. Rom 8:19-21; Col 1:18-20).

B. The Mission of the Church

34. It is God's design to gather all creation under the Lordship of Christ (cf. Eph 1:10), and to bring humanity and all creation into communion. As a reflection of the communion in the Triune God, the Church is God's instrument in fulfilling this goal. The Church is called to manifest God's mercy to humanity, and to bring humanity to its purpose – to praise and glorify God together with all the heavenly hosts. The mission of the Church is to serve the purpose of God as a gift given to the world in order that all may believe (cf. Jn 17:21).

35. As persons who acknowledge Jesus Christ as Lord and Saviour, Christians are called to proclaim the Gospel in word and deed. They are to address those who have not heard, as well as those who are no longer living

according to the Gospel, the Good News of the reign of God. They are called to live its values and to be a foretaste of that reign in the world. Mission thus belongs to the very being of the Church. This is a central implication of affirming the apostolicity of the Church, which is inseparable from the other three attributes of the Church – unity, holiness and catholicity. All four attributes relate both to the nature of God's own being and to the practical demands of authentic mission.[11] If in the life of the Church, any of them is impaired, the Church's mission is compromised.

36. The Church, embodying in its own life the mystery of salvation and the transfiguration of humanity, participates in the mission of Christ to reconcile all things to God and to one another through Christ (cf. 2 Cor 5:18-21; Rom 8:18-25). Through its worship (leitourgia); service, which includes the stewardship of creation (diakonia); and proclamation (kerygma) the Church participates in and points to the reality of the Kingdom of God. In the power of the Holy Spirit the Church testifies to the divine mission in which the Father sent the Son to be the Saviour of the world.

37. In exercising its mission, the Church cannot be true to itself without giving witness (martyria) to God's will for the salvation and transformation of the world. That is why it started at once preaching the Word, bearing witness to the great deeds of God and inviting everyone to repentance (metanoia), baptism (cf. Acts 2:37-38) and the fuller life that is enjoyed by the followers of Jesus (cf. Jn 10:10).

38. As Christ's mission encompassed the preaching of the Word of God and the commitment to care for those suffering and in need, so the apostolic Church in its mission from the beginning combined preaching of the Word, the call to repentance, faith, baptism and diakonia. This the Church understands as an essential dimension of

its identity. The Church in this way signifies, participates in, and anticipates the new humanity God wants, and also serves to proclaim God's grace in human situations and needs until Christ comes in glory (cf. Mt 25:31).

39. Because the servanthood of Christ entails suffering it is evident (as expressed in the New Testament writings) that the witness (martyria) of the Church will entail – for both individuals and for the community – the way of the cross, even to the point of martyrdom (cf. Mt 10:16-33; 16:24-28).

40. The Church is called and empowered to share the suffering of all by advocacy and care for the poor, the needy and the marginalised. This entails critically analysing and exposing unjust structures, and working for their transformation. The Church is called to proclaim the words of hope and comfort of the Gospel, by its works of compassion and mercy (cf. Lk.4:18-19). This faithful witness may involve Christians themselves in suffering for the sake of the Gospel. The Church is called to heal and reconcile broken human relationships and to be God's instrument in the reconciliation of human division and hatred (cf. 2Cor. 5:18-21). It is also called, together with all people of goodwill, to care for the integrity of creation in addressing the abuse and destruction of God's creation, and to participate in God's healing of broken relationships between creation and humanity.

41. In the power of the Holy Spirit, the Church is called to proclaim faithfully the whole teaching of Christ and to share the Good News of the Kingdom – that is, the totality of apostolic faith, life and witness – with everyone throughout the entire world. Thus the Church seeks faithfully to proclaim and live the love of God for all, and to fulfil Christ's mission for the salvation and transformation of the world, to the glory of God.

42. God restores and enriches communion with humanity, granting eternal life in God's Triune Being.

Through redeemed humanity the whole world is meant to be drawn to the goal of restoration and salvation. This divine plan reaches its fulfilment in the new heaven and the new earth (cf. Rev 21:1) in God's holy Kingdom.

C. The Church as Sign and Instrument of God's Intention and Plan for the World

43. The one, holy, catholic and apostolic Church is sign and instrument of God's intention and plan for the whole world. Already participating in the love and life of God, the Church is a prophetic sign which points beyond itself to the purpose of all creation, the fulfilment of the Kingdom of God. For this reason Jesus called his followers the "salt of the earth", "the light of the world" and "a city built on a hill" (Mt 5:13-16).

44. Aware of God's saving presence in the world, the Church already praises and glorifies the Triune God through worship and discipleship, and serves God's plan. Yet the Church does so not only for itself, but rather renders praise and thanks on behalf of all peoples for God's grace and the forgiveness of sins.

45. To acknowledge the nature of the Church as "mysterion" (cf. Eph 1:9-10; 5:32) indicates the transcendent character of its God-given reality as one, holy, catholic and apostolic. The Church can never be fully and unequivocally grasped only in its visible appearance. Therefore the visible organisational structures of the Church must always be seen and judged, for good or ill, in the light of God's gifts of salvation in Christ, celebrated in the Liturgy (cf. Heb 12:18-24).

46. As instrument of God's plan the Church is the community of people called by God and sent as Christ's disciples to proclaim the Good News in word and deed, that the world may believe (cf. Lk 24:46-49). Thus it makes present throughout history "the tender mercy of our God" (Lk. 1:78).

47. Sent as Christ's disciples, the people of God must witness to and participate in God's reconciliation, healing, and transformation of creation. The integrity of the Church as God's instrument is at stake in witness through proclamation, and concrete actions in union with all people of goodwill, for the sake of justice, peace, and the integrity of creation.

II. The Church in History

A. The Church *in via*

48. The Church is an eschatological reality, already anticipating the Kingdom. However, the Church on earth is not yet the full visible realisation of the Kingdom. Being also an historical reality, it is exposed to the ambiguities of all human history and therefore needs constant repentance and renewal in order to respond fully to its vocation.

Church as "Sacrament"?

Although all churches agree that the church is a sign and instrument, some churches express their understanding of the reality of the church in Sacramental terms; some speak of the church as Sacrament; others do not normally use this language, or reject it outright.

The churches who use the expression "Church as Sacrament" do so because they understand the Church as an effective sign of what God wishes for the world: namely, the communion of all together and with the Triune God, the joy for which God created the world (notwithstanding the sinfulness of Christians).

The churches who do not use the concept of Sacrament for the Church do not do so for at least two reasons, namely (1) the need for a clear distinction between the Church and Sacraments: the Sacraments are the means of salvation through which Christ sustains the Church, and not actions by which the Church realises or actualises itself; and (2) the use of the word "Sacrament" for the Church obscures the fact that, for them, the Church is a sign and instrument of God's intention and plan – but it is so as a communion which, while being holy, is still subject to sin.

Behind this lack of agreement lie varying views about the instrumentality of the Church with regard to salvation. Yet those who have become accustomed to call the Church "Sacrament" would still distinguish between the ways in which baptism and the Lord's Supper on the one hand, and the Church on the other, are signs and instruments of God's plan. And those who do not use the phrase "Church as Sacrament" would still uphold that the Church is God's holy instrument for his divine purpose (cf. next box, following §56).

49. On the one hand, the Church already participates in the communion of God, in faith, hope, love, and glorification of God's name, and lives as a communion of redeemed persons. Because of the presence of the Spirit and of the Word of God, the Church – as Creatura Verbi and Creatura Spiritus (cf. §10ff.), as the communion of all believers held in personal relationship with God by God himself (cf. §11), as the people of God (cf. §§19-20) – is already the eschatological community God wills.

50. On the other hand the Church, in its human dimension, is made up of human beings who – though they are members of the body of Christ and open to the free activity of the Holy Spirit (cf. Jn 3:8) in illuminating hearts and binding consciences – are still subject to the conditions of the world. Therefore the Church is affected by these conditions. It is exposed to:

- change, which allows for both positive development and growth as well as for the negative possibility of decline and distortion;
- individual, cultural and historical conditioning which can contribute to a richness of insights and expressions of faith, but also to relativising tendencies or to absolutising particular views;
- the power of sin.

51. One particularly striking experience of human weakness and failure that has afflicted the Christian community in via is the sometimes widespread discrepancy between membership in the church, on the one hand, and vibrant profession and practice of the Christian faith, on the other. Many of our communities face the challenge that some of their members seem to "belong without believing", while other individuals opt out of Church membership, claiming that they can, with greater authenticity, "believe without belonging". The challenge of living our faith as believing communities in such a way that all those who belong are seriously committed Christians, and all who sincerely believe want to belong, is a challenge that we share; it crosses the lines which divide us.

52. The oneness, holiness, catholicity and apostolicity of the Church are God's gifts and are essential attributes of the Church's nature and mission. However, there is a continual tension in the historical life of the Church between that which is already given and that which is not yet fully realised.

53. The essential oneness which belongs to the very nature of the Church, and is already given to it in Jesus Christ, stands in contrast to the actual divisions within and between the churches. Yet in spite of all divisions the unity given to the Church is already manifest in the one Gospel present in all churches, and appears in many features of their lives (cf. Eph 4:4-5; 1 Tim 2:5; Acts 4:12). The unfortunate divisions among the churches are due partly to sin, and partly to a sincere attempt of Christians to be faithful to the truth. Working for the unity of the Church means working for fuller visible embodiment of the oneness that belongs to its nature.

54. The essential holiness of the Church stands in contrast to sin, individual as well as communal. This holiness is witnessed to in every generation in the lives of holy men and women, as well as in the holy words the Church

proclaims and the holy acts it performs in the name of God, the All-Holy. Nevertheless, in the course of the Church's history sin has again and again disfigured its witness, and run counter to the Church's true nature and vocation. Therefore in the Church there has been again and again God's ever-new offer of forgiveness, together with the call for repentance, renewal and reform. Responding to this call means fuller visible embodiment of the holiness that belongs to its nature.

55. The essential catholicity of the Church is confronted with divisions between and within the Christian communities regarding their life and preaching of the Gospel. Its catholicity transcends all barriers and proclaims God's word to all peoples: where the whole mystery of Christ is present, there too is the Church catholic. However, the catholicity of the Church is challenged by the fact that the integrity of the Gospel is not adequately preached to all; the fullness of communion is not offered to all. Nevertheless, the Spirit given to the Church is the Spirit of the Lordship of Christ over all creation and all times. The Church is called to remove all obstacles to the full embodiment of what is already its nature by the power of the Holy Spirit.

56. The essential apostolicity of the Church stands in contrast to shortcomings and errors of the churches in their proclamation of the Word of God. Nevertheless, this apostolicity is witnessed to in the many ways in which the Church, under the guidance of the Holy Spirit, has been faithful to the testimony of the apostles concerning Jesus Christ. The Church is called to return continuously to the apostolic truth and to be renewed in its worship and mission stemming from its apostolic origin (cf. Acts 2:42-47). By doing so it makes visible, and does justice to, the apostolic Gospel which is already given to it and works in it in the Spirit, making it the Church.

The Church and Sin

All the churches agree that there is sin, corporate and individual, in the Church's history (cf. Rev 2:2). Yet they differ as to how this reality should be understood and expressed.

For some, it is impossible to say "the Church sins" because they see the Church as a gift of God, sharing in God's holiness. The Church is the spotless bride of Christ (cf. Eph 5:25-27); it is a communion in the Holy Spirit, the holy people of God, justified by grace through faith in Christ (cf. Rom 3:22; Eph 2:8-9). As such, the Church cannot sin. The gift is lived out in fragile human beings who are liable to sin, but the sins of the members of the Church are not the sins of the Church. The Church is rather the locus of salvation and healing (cf. Is 53; Lk 4:18-19). According to this perspective one can, and must, speak only of the sin of the members of the Church and of groups within the Church, a situation described by the parable of the wheat and the chaff (cf. Mt 13:24-30), and by the Augustinian formula of *corpus permixtum*.

Others, while they too state that the Church, as the creature of God's Word and Spirit, the body of Christ, is holy and without sin, say at the same time that it does sin. They say this because they define the Church as the communion of its members who – although they are justified believers brought to birth by the Spirit, and Christ's own body – in this world are still sinful human beings (cf. 1 Jn 1:8-10).

Yet others believe that while one cannot speak of the sins of the Church, sin in the Church may become systemic and also affect the institution.

While there are these different understandings concerning the Church and sin, we ask whether all churches might not be able to agree on the following proposition:

The relationship between sin and holiness in the Church is not a relationship of two equal realities, because sin and holiness do not exist on the same level. Rather, holiness denotes the Church's nature and God's will for it, while sinfulness is contrary to both (cf. 1 Cor 15:21-26).

B. In Christ – But Not Yet in Full Communion

57. One blessing of the ecumenical movement has been the gradual and increasing discovery of the many aspects of life in Christ which our still-divided churches share; we all participate in some way in Jesus Christ, although we do not yet live in full communion with each other. Such divisions among the churches hinder the mission of the Church. Not only does mission have as its ultimate goal the koinonia of all; but effective mission is thwarted by the scandal of division: Jesus prayed that all his disciples be one precisely "so that the world may believe" (Jn 17:21). Thus mission is essentially related to the very being of the Church as koinonia (cf. 1 Jn 1:1-3). This is why the restoration of unity between Christians, brought about through committed dialogue about issues that still divide them as well as through the continual renewal of their lives, is such an urgent task.

58. Growth in communion between our churches unfolds within the setting of that wider communion between Christians which extends back into the past and forward into the future. By the power of the Holy Spirit the Church lives in communion with Christ Jesus, in whom all in heaven and earth are joined in the communion of God the Holy One: this is the communion of the saints. The final destiny of the Church is to be caught up

in the intimate relation of Father, Son and Holy Spirit, to praise and to enjoy God forever (cf. Rev 7:9-10; 22:1-5).

59. There remains by virtue of creation a natural bond between human beings and between humanity and creation. "So if anyone is in Christ, there is a new creation" (2 Cor 5:17). The new life of communion builds upon and transforms, but never wholly replaces, what was first given in creation; within history, it never completely overcomes the distortions of the relationship between human beings caused by sin. Sharing in Christ is often restricted and only partially realised. The new life therefore entails the constant need for repentance, mutual forgiveness and restoration. It belongs to the essence of fellowship with God that the members of Christ's body pray day after day "Forgive us our sins" (Lk 11:4; cf. Mt 6:12). But the Father cleanses us from our sins in the blood of his son Jesus and, if we acknowledge our sins, we will be forgiven (cf. 1 Jn 1:7-10). Nonetheless, there is a genuine enjoyment of new life here and now and a confident anticipation of sharing in the fullness of communion in the life to come.

C. Communion and Diversity

60. Diversity in unity and unity in diversity are gifts of God to the Church. Through the Holy Spirit God bestows diverse and complementary gifts on all the faithful for the common good, for service within the community and to the world (cf. 1 Cor 12:7 and 2 Cor 9:13). No one is self-sufficient. The disciples are called to be one, while enriched by their diversities – fully united, while respectful of the diversity of persons and community groups (cf. Acts 2; 15; Eph 2:15-16).

61. There is a rich diversity of Christian life and witness born out of the diversity of cultural and historical context. The Gospel has to be rooted and lived authentically in each and every place. It has to be proclaimed in language, symbols and images that engage with, and are

relevant to, particular times and particular contexts. The communion of the Church demands the constant inter-play of cultural expressions of the Gospel if the riches of the Gospel are to be appreciated for the whole people of God.[12] Problems are created

- when one culture seeks to capture the Gospel and claims to be the one and only authentic way of cele-brating the Gospel;
- when one culture seeks to impose its expression of the Gospel on others as the only authentic expression of the Gospel;
- when one culture finds it impossible to recognise the Gospel being faithfully proclaimed in another cul-ture.

62. Authentic diversity in the life of communion must not be stifled: authentic unity must not be surrendered. Each local church must be the place where two things are simultaneously guaranteed: the safeguarding of unity and the flourishing of a legitimate diversity. There are limits within which diversity is an enrichment but out-side of which diversity is not only unacceptable, but destructive of the gift of unity. Similarly unity, particular-ly when it tends to be identified with uniformity, can be destructive of authentic diversity and thus can become unacceptable. Through shared faith in Christ, expressed in the proclamation of the Word, celebration of the Sacraments and lives of service and witness, each local Christian community participates in the life and witness of all Christian communities in all places and all times. A pastoral ministry for the service of unity and the uphold-ing of diversity is one of the many charisms given to the Church. It helps to keep those with different gifts and perspectives mutually accountable to each other within the communion.

63. Diversity is not the same as division. Within the Church, divisions (heresies and schisms), as well as polit-

ical conflicts and expressions of hatred, threaten God's gift of communion. Christians are called to work untiringly to overcome divisions, to prevent legitimate diversities from becoming causes of division, and to live a life of diversities reconciled.

Limits of Diversity?

While all recognise the wide range of diversity in the Church, there is often a tendency (conscious or unconscious) to give more value to some aspects of this diversity than others. This is especially true with regard to diversity in our position on particular issues, e.g. diversity in our worship.

(a) Diversities in expression of the Gospel, in words and in actions can enrich life in communion. Particular emphases today are carried in the life and witness of different churches. How far are the different emphases conflicting positions, or rather an expression of legitimate diversity? Does the weight placed upon the different emphases obscure the fullness of the Gospel message?

(b) What weight do Christians place on ecclesial and confessional identity? For some the preservation of such identity, for the foreseeable future or even permanently, and even within a life of koinonia, is necessary for safeguarding particular truths and rich legitimate diversities that belong to a life of communion. Others understand the goal of visible communion as beyond particular ecclesial or confessional identities – a communion in which the riches safeguarded by confessional traditions are brought together in the witness and experience of a common faith and life. For others the model of "reconciled diversity" remains a compelling one. Most, however, agree that an openness is required about the unity to which God calls us; and that as we move by steps, under the guidance of

38

the Holy Spirit (cf. Jn 16:13), the portrait of visible unity will become clearer. Churches understand their relation to the one, holy, catholic and apostolic Church in different ways. This has a bearing upon the way they relate to other churches and their perception of the road to visible unity.

(c) In order for the Churches to move further towards complete mutual recognition and full communion, they need to reflect on how they understand and claim their own ecclesial identity and how they regard the ecclesial status of other churches and other Christians.

One type of Ecclesiology identifies the Church exclusively with one's own community, dismissing other communities or persons which claim churchly status into an ecclesiological void. According to a modified form of this type, other communities may possess elements of the Church which bring those who enjoy them into a real, though imperfect, communion outside of one's own community. Another variant of this type offers a pneumatological account of the existence of Christian life outside the bounds of one's own community – something which is nevertheless, identified as the Church.

A second type of ecclesiology, while claiming for its own community a full place in the Church catholic, allows equal status to some other communities (even though the degree and mode of communion actually existing between it and them may vary). One variant of this approach is the so-called "branch theory", or *tropoi* theory, used to describe the situation of the different Churches. Another variant is "denominationalism", which allows for a quite broad spectrum of churches to coexist in organisational independence while constituting, in aggregate, "the Church universal". A further variant is called "cultural families of churches", each of equal value.

A third type of ecclesiology neither identifies one's own community with the One Church, nor does it speak of elements or different degrees of fullness of the Church; yet it does not place all ecclesial bodies on the same level, either. It states rather that the One Church of Christ exists wherever the Gospel is rightly proclaimed and the sacraments are duly administered, because Christ is present and at work wherever these means of his grace are present. However, according to this position there is a difference between historical church bodies as regards the correspondence between their official practice and teaching, on the one hand, and the Gospel present with in them, on the other. Whereas in some churches there is such a correspondence, in other churches the Gospel is enveloped in official teachings and practices that contradict it. According to this view even such contradictions, as long as those means of Christ's grace are recognisably there, cannot prevent his presence; nor do they nullify the belonging to his body, the One Church. But they do establish a difference in rank and status between these historic churches which has to be overcome.

(d) One of the pressing ecumenical questions is whether and how churches, at this stage of the ecumenical movement, can live in mutual accountability so that they can sustain one another in unity and legitimate diversity, and can prevent new issues from becoming causes of division within and between churches.

D. The Church as Communion of Local Churches

64. From the beginning contact was maintained between local churches by collections, exchanges of letters, visits and tangible expressions of solidarity (cf. 1 Cor 16; 2 Cor 8:1-9; Gal 2:9ff; etc.). From time to time, during the first centuries, local churches assembled to take coun-

sel together. All of these were ways of nurturing interdependence and maintaining communion.

65. The communion of the Church is expressed in the communion between local churches, in each of which the fullness of the Church resides. The communion of the Church embraces local churches in each place and all places at all times. Local churches are held in the communion of the Church by the one Gospel,[13] the one baptism and the one Lord's Supper, served by a common ministry. This communion of local churches is thus not an optional extra, but is an essential aspect of what it means to be the Church.

66. The communion of local churches is sustained by the living elements of apostolicity and catholicity: Scripture, baptism, communion and the service of a common ministry. As "bonds of communion" these gifts serve the authentic continuity of the life of the whole Church and help to sustain the local churches in a communion of truth and love. They are given to maintain the Church in integrity as the one Church of Jesus Christ, the same yesterday, today and tomorrow. The goal of the search for full communion is realised when all the churches are able to recognise in one another the one, holy, catholic and apostolic Church in all its fullness. This full communion will be expressed on the local and universal levels through conciliar forms of life and action. In such a communion of unity and authentic diversities, churches are bound in all aspects of their life together at all levels in confessing the one faith and engaging in worship and witness, deliberation and action.

Local Church

The term "local church" is used differently by different traditions. For some traditions the "local" church is the congregation of believers gathered in one place to hear the Word and celebrate the Sacraments. For others, "local" or "particular" church refers to the bishop with the people around the bishop, gathered to hear the Word and celebrate the Sacraments. In some churches the term "local church" is used of both the diocese and of the parish. At another level, "local church" can refer to several dioceses or to regional churches gathered together in a synodal structure under a presidency.

There are different ecclesiological concepts behind these usages, yet most Churches agree that each local church, however it is defined, is united to every other in the universal Church and contains within it the fullness of what it is to be the Church. There is often a discrepancy between theological description of local church and how the local church is experienced by the faithful.

III. The Life of Communion
in and for the World

67. God gives to the Church all the gifts and resources needed for its life and mission in and for the world. God bestows on it the grace of the apostolic faith, baptism and Eucharist as means of grace to create and sustain the koinonia. These and other means serve to animate the people of God in their proclamation of the Kingdom and in their participation in the promises of God.

A. Apostolic Faith

68. The Church is called at all times and in all places to "continue in the apostles' teaching" (Acts 2:42). The faith "once for all entrusted to the saints" (Jude v. 3) is the faith of the Church through the ages.

69. The revealed apostolic faith is uniquely witnessed to in Scripture. This faith is articulated in the Nicene-Constantinopolitan Creed (381).[14] The Church is called upon to proclaim the same faith in each generation, in each and every place. Each church in its place is challenged in the power of the Holy Spirit to make that faith relevant and alive in its particular cultural, social, political and religious context. While the apostolic faith has to be interpreted in the context of changing times and places,[15] it must be in continuity with the original witness of the apostolic community and with the faithful explication of that witness throughout the ages.

70. The apostolic faith does not refer to one fixed formula or to a specific phase in Christian history. The faith transmitted through the living tradition of the Church is the faith evoked by the Word of God, inspired by the Holy Spirit and attested in Scripture. Its content is set forth in the Creeds of the Early Church and also testified to in other forms. It is proclaimed in many Confessions of Faith of the churches. It is preached throughout the world today. It is articulated in Canons and Books of Discipline from many periods and stages in the lives of the churches. Thus the apostolic faith is confessed in worship, in life,

service and mission – in the living traditions of the Church.

71. The apostolic tradition of the Church is the continuity in the permanent characteristics of the Church of the apostles: witness to the apostolic faith, proclamation and fresh interpretation of the Gospel, celebration of baptism and Eucharist, the transmission of ministerial responsibilities, communion in prayer, love, joy and suffering, service to the sick and needy, communion among the local churches and sharing the divine gifts which have been given to each.

72. Within the apostolic tradition the Nicene-Constantinopolitan Creed, promulgated by the Early Ecumenical Councils, is a pre-eminent expression of the apostolic faith. Although its language, like that of all texts, is conditioned by time and context, it has been the Creed most widely used by Christians throughout the centuries and remains so today throughout the world. The fact that some churches do not explicitly use this Creed liturgically or catechetically need not be interpreted as a sign of their departure from the apostolic faith. Nevertheless the existence of such differences suggests that churches need to be attentive to the tolerable limits to diversity in confessing one faith.

73. The faith of the Church has to be lived out in active response to the challenges of every age and place. It speaks to personal and social situations, including situations of injustice, of violation of human dignity and of the degradation of creation. For example, when Christians confess that God is creator of all, they recognise the goodness of creation and commit themselves to care for the well-being of humanity and for all that God has made. When Christians confess Christ crucified and risen, they commit themselves to witness to the paschal mystery in word and deed. When Christians confess the Holy Spirit as Lord and Giver of Life, they know themselves to be

already citizens of heaven and they commit themselves to discern the Spirit's gift in their lives. When Christians confess the one, holy, catholic and apostolic Church, they commit themselves to manifest and promote the realisation of these attributes.[16]

B. Baptism

74. In the Nicene-Constantinopolitan Creed Christians confess "one baptism for the remission of sins". Through Baptism with water in the name of the Triune God, Father, Son and Holy Spirit, Christians are united with Christ, with each other and with the Church of every time and place. Baptism is thus a basic bond of unity. The recognition of the one baptism into Christ constitutes an urgent call to the churches to overcome their divisions and visibly manifest their communion in faith and through mutual accountability in all aspects of Christian life and witness.

75. Baptism is the celebration of new life through Christ and of participation in the baptism, life, death and resurrection of Jesus Christ (cf. Mt 3:13-17; Rom 6:3-5). Baptism involves confession of sin, conversion of heart, pardoning, cleansing and sanctification. It is the gift of the Holy Spirit, incorporation into the Body of Christ, participation in the Kingdom of God and the life of the world to come (cf. Eph 2:6). Baptism consecrates the believer as a member of "a chosen race, a royal priesthood, a holy nation" (1 Peter 2:9).

76. "Baptism is related not only to momentary experience, but to life-long growth into Christ".[17] Nourished by the worship, witness and teaching of the Church, the believer grows in his or her relationship with Christ, and with other members of the body of Christ. In this process the faith of the believer – whether he or she was baptised as an infant, or upon personal profession of faith – is nourished by, and tested against, the faith of the Church.[18]

77. All human beings have in common their creation at God's hand, and God's providential care for them; and they share in social, economic and cultural institutions which preserve human life. As people are baptised they are clothed in Christ (cf. Gal 3:27), they enter into the koinonia of Christ's Body (cf. 1 Cor 12:13), they receive the Holy Spirit which is the privilege of God's adopted children (cf. Rom 8:15f), and so they enjoy, in anticipation, that participation in the divine nature which God promises and wills for humankind (cf. 2 Pet 1:4). In the present, the solidarity of Christians with the joys and sorrows of their neighbours, and their engagement in the struggle for the dignity of all who suffer, for the excluded and the poor, belongs to their baptismal vocation. It is the way they are brought face to face with Christ in his identification with the victimised and outcast.

Baptism

Although BEM and the churches' responses to it registered a high degree of agreement about baptism, some significant issues remain:[19]

(a) the difference between churches which baptise infants, and those which baptise only those able to offer a personal profession of faith;

(b) the inability of some churches to recognise baptism performed by others, and the related practice of "re"-baptism;

(c) the different starting points and historical development of the terms "ordinance" and "Sacrament" (although both are understood as describing the act by which people are brought to new life in Christ);

46

(d) whether baptism is best understood as effecting the reality of new life in Christ, or as reflecting it;

(e) the difference between the churches which baptise insisting on the Trinitarian formula according to the command of Jesus (Mt 28: 19-20), and those which insist that baptism "in the name of Jesus Christ" is more consistent with the practice of the apostles (cf. Acts 2:38);

(f) the difference between churches which employ water as the instrument of baptism, and those which believe that Christian baptism does not require any such material instrument;

(g) those communities which believe that baptism with water is necessary, and those which do not celebrate baptism, yet understand themselves as sharing in the spiritual experience of life in Christ.

C. Eucharist

78. Communion established in baptism is focused and brought to expression in the Eucharist. There is a dynamic connection between baptism and Eucharist. Baptismal faith is re-affirmed and grace given for the faithful living out of the Christian calling.

79. The Lord's Supper is the celebration where, gathered around his table, Christians receive the body and blood of Christ. It is a proclamation of the Gospel, a glorification of the Father for everything accomplished in creation, redemption and sanctification (doxologia); a memorial of the death and resurrection of Christ Jesus and what was accomplished once for all on the Cross (anamnesis); an invocation of the Holy Spirit (epiclesis); an intercession; the communion of the faithful and an anticipation and foretaste of the kingdom to come.

80. In 1 Corinthians 10 and 11, Paul highlights the connection between the Lord's Supper and the nature of the Church. "The cup of blessing that we bless, is it not a sharing in the blood of Christ? The bread that we break, is it not a sharing in the body of Christ? Because there is one bread, we who are many are one body, for we all partake of the one bread" (1 Cor 10:16-17). He also draws attention to the moral implications of the celebration: "Examine yourselves, and only then eat of the bread and drink of the cup" (1 Cor 11:28).

81. Just as the confession of faith and baptism are inseparable from a life of service and witness, so too the Mass demands reconciliation and sharing among all those regarded as brothers and sisters in the one family of God and is a constant challenge in the search for appropriate relationships in social, economic and political life (cf. Mt 5:23ff; 1 Cor 10:14; 1 Cor 11:20-22). Because the Lord's Supper is the Sacrament which builds up community, all kinds of injustice, racism, estrangement, and lack of freedom are radically challenged when we share in the body and blood of Christ. Through Holy Communion the all-renewing grace of God penetrates the human personality and restores human dignity. The Eucharist, therefore, obliges us also to participate actively in the ongoing restoration of the world's situation and the human condition. God's judgement demands that our behaviour be consistent with the reconciling presence of God in human history.

Eucharist

Although BEM and the responses to it from the churches registered a degree of agreement about the Eucharist, significant differences remain:

As regards the understanding and practice of the Eucharist there remains the question whether it is primarily a meal where Christians receive the body and blood of Christ, or primarily a service of thanksgiving.

Among those for whom the Eucharist is primarily a service of thanksgiving, there is growing convergence concerning its sacrificial character. Remaining disagreement centres principally on the questions of how the sacrifice of Jesus Christ on Calvary is made present in the Eucharistic act. A help in reconciling the different approaches has been made by the use of biblical and patristic scholarship to probe more deeply into the meaning of the biblical term anamnesis. However, some maintain that the concept has been made to bear more weight in theological and ecumenical texts than it is capable of bearing.

Churches continue to disagree about the nature and mode of the presence of Christ in the Eucharist. Some important differences remain regarding the role and invocation of the Holy Spirit in the whole eucharistic celebration.

It is a matter of continuing concern that not all Christians share the communion. Some churches believe that eucharistic sharing is both a means of building communion between divided churches as well as its goal; others either do not offer Eucharistic hospitality, or offer it under restricted conditions. Some churches invite all who believe in Jesus Christ to receive communion; other Churches invite only those who believe in Jesus Christ and are baptised and in good standing in their own Churches. Among still other churches eucharistic communion is understood as the ultimate expression of agreement in faith and of a communion in life. Such an understandng would make the sharing of the Lord's Supper with those outside their own tradition an anomaly. As a result, for some churches the practice of "Eucharistic hospitality" is the antithesis of the commitment to full visible unity.

Behind the variety of practices lie serious theological problems that are at present unresolved. While recent bilateral and multilateral theological dialogues have achieved much in overcoming some of these traditional disagreements, it is evident that there is a continuing need for growth in understanding concerning the actual faith and practice of the divided churches.

D. Ministry of All the Faithful

82. The Church is called at all times and in all places to serve God after the example of the Lord who came to serve rather than to be served. The idea of service is central to any biblical understanding of ministry.

83. Every Christian receives gifts of the Holy Spirit for the upbuilding of the Church, and for his or her part in the mission of Christ. These gifts are given for the common good (cf. 1 Cor 12:7), and place obligations of responsibility and mutual accountability on every individual and local community, and indeed on the Church as a whole at every level of its life. Strengthened by the Spirit, Christians are called to live out their discipleship in a variety of forms of service. The teaching of the faith and of its moral implications is entrusted in a special way to parents, although all the faithful are called upon to witness to the Gospel in word and deed. Catechists and theologians provide an invaluable service in handing on and deepening our understanding of the faith. The following of Christ, who came to bring good news to the poor and healing to the sick (cf. Luke 4: 18-19), provides a powerful and specifically Christian motivation for believers to

engage in other forms of service: education and health care, charitable assistance to the poor and the promotion of justice, peace and the protection of the environment.

84. Through their participation in Christ, the unique priest of the new covenant (cf. Heb 9:11), Christians are constituted a royal priesthood called to offer spiritual sacrifices (cf. 1 Pet 2). and indeed their very selves as a living sacrifice (cf. Rom 12:1) after the example of Jesus himself. This calling underlies the Church's potentially costly witness to justice and the duty of intercession.

85. In this way every Christian, on the basis of the one baptism into Christ, should seek to serve the world by proclaiming good news to the poor, "release to the captives and recovery of sight to the blind" and setting at liberty those who are oppressed. In short, this is an obligation resting equally on all "to proclaim the year of the Lord's favour" in all the varied situations of need in the world throughout the ages (Lk 4:18-19).

E. Ministry of the Ordained

86. In calling and sending the Twelve and his other apostles, Jesus laid foundations for the ongoing proclamation of the Kingdom and the service of the community of his disciples. Faithful to his example, from the earliest times there were those chosen by the community under the guidance of the Spirit, and given specific authority and responsibility. Ordained ministers serve in the building up of the community, in equipping the saints, and in strengthening the Church's witness in the world (cf. Eph 4:12-13). They may not dispense with the ongoing support and the encouragement of the community – for whom they are chosen, and for whom they are empowered by the Holy Spirit to act as representative persons. Ordained ministers have a special responsibility for the ministry of Word and Sacrament. They have a ministry of pastoral care, teaching and leadership in mis-

sion. In all of those ways they strengthen the communion in faith, life and witness of the whole people of God.

87. There is no single pattern of conferring ministry in the New Testament. The Spirit has at different times led the Church to adapt its ministries to contextual needs; various forms of the ordained ministry have been blessed with gifts of the Spirit. The threefold ministry of bishop, presbyter and deacon had become by the third century the generally accepted pattern. It is still retained by many churches today, though subsequently it underwent considerable changes in its practical exercise and is still changing in most churches today. Other churches have developed different patterns of ministry.

88. The chief responsibility of the ordained ministry is to assemble and build up the Body of Christ by proclaiming and teaching the Word of God, by celebrating baptism and the Eucharist and by guiding the life of the community in its worship, its mission and its service. Essential to its testimony are not merely its words, but the love of its members for one another, the quality of their service to those in need, a just and disciplined life and a fair exercise of power and authority.

89. In the course of history, the Church has developed several means for maintaining its apostolicity through time, in different circumstances and cultural contexts: the scriptural canon, dogma, liturgical order, structures wider than the level of local communities. The ministry of the ordained is to serve in a specific way the apostolic continuity of the Church as a whole. In this context, succession in ministry is a means of serving the apostolic continuity of the Church. This is focused in the act of ordination when the Church as a whole, through its ordained ministers, takes part in the act of ordaining those chosen for the ministry of Word and Sacrament.

Ordained Ministry

Although BEM and the responses to it, multilateral and bilateral dialogues, and church union processes have identified the points of convergence on the subject of ordained ministry there remain issues to be explored further:

(a) the location of the ministry of the ordained in, with, among or over the people of God;

(b) Eucharistic presidency;

(c) the threefold ministry as a means to and expression of unity;

(d) the Sacrament of ordination;

(e) the restriction of ordination to the ministry of Word and Sacrament to men only;

(f) the relationship between the apostolic succession of ministry and the apostolic continuity of the Church as a whole;

(g) the ways in which ordination is considered constitutive of the Church.

F. Oversight: Personal, Communal, Collegial

90. The Church, as the body of Christ and the eschatological people of God, is built up by the Holy Spirit through a diversity of gifts or ministries. This diversity calls for a ministry of co-ordination so that these gifts may enrich the whole Church, its unity and mission. The faithful exercise of the ministry of episkopé under the Gospel is a requirement of fundamental importance for the Church's life and mission. The responsibility of those called to exercise oversight cannot be fulfilled without the collaboration, support and assent of the whole community. At the same time, the effective and faithful life of the

community is served by a ministry of leadership set apart to guide its mission, teaching and common life.

91. In the course of the first centuries, communion between local congregations – which had been maintained by a series of informal links such as visits, letters and collections – became more and more expressed in institutional forms. The purpose was to hold the local congregations in communion, to safeguard and hand on apostolic truth, to give mutual support and to lead in witnessing to the Gospel. All these functions are summed up in the term episkopé.

92. The specific development of structures of episkopé varied in different regions of the Church: this was true of both the collegial expression of episkopé in synods, and its personal embodiment in the individual bishops. The crystallisation of most of the episcopal functions in the hands of one individual (episkopos) came later in some places than in others. What is evident in every case is that episkopé and episcopacy are in the service of maintaining continuity in apostolic truth and unity of life.

93. In the 16th century, oversight came to be exercised in a variety of ways in the churches which took their identity through the continental Reformation. These Reformers, seeking to return to the apostolicity of the Church which they considered to have been corrupted, saw themselves faced with the alternative of either staying within the inherited church structures or remaining faithful to the apostolicity of the Church, and thus accepted a break with the overall structure of the Church, including the ministry of universal primacy. Nevertheless, they continued to see the need for a ministry of episkopé, which the churches which went through the Reformation ordered in different ways. Some exercised episkopé in synodal forms. Others kept or developed ministries of personal episkopé, including, for some, the sign of historic episcopal succession.

Episkopé, Bishops and Apostolic Succession

One of the most difficult issues dividing Christian communities concerns this form of ministry and its relation to the apostolicity of the Church. To focus the question in a very precise way: churches remain divided about whether the historic episcopate – in the sense of bishops ordained in apostolic succession back to the earliest generations of the Church – is a necessary component of ecclesial order as intended by Christ for his community; or is merely one form of church structure which, because it is so traditional, is particularly advantageous for today's community but is not essential. Still other communities see no special reason for privileging episcopal structure, or even believe it is better avoided, for they see it as prone to abuse.

Ecumenical reflection on the more general concept of a ministry of episkopé, as described in the preceding paragraphs, has helped to bring to light hitherto unrecognised parallels between episcopal and non-episcopal churches in the way oversight is exercised. Moreover, both types of churches have been able to acknowledge a degree of apostolicity in one another, even though disagreement about the need for bishops remains.

94. Through the commissioned functions of the ordained ministry, Word, Sacrament and discipline, God not only furthers the announcement of his Kingdom but also discloses its fulfilment. This underlies that aspect of ministry known as episkopé, which means both oversight and visitation. Like every other aspect of ministry, episkopé both belongs to the whole church and is entrusted as a particular charge on specific persons. For this reason it is frequently stressed that, at every level of the Church's life, the ministry must be exercised in personal,

communal and collegial ways. It should be remembered that "personal", "communal" and "collegial" refer not only to particular structures and processes, but also describe the informal reality of the bonds of koinonia, the mutual belonging and accountability within the ongoing common life of the Church.

(I) PERSONAL

95. Through the discernment of the community and under the guidance of the Holy Spirit, God calls out persons for the exercise of the ministry of oversight. Episkopé is not to be understood as a function only of these ministers who are in many churches designated bishops. Oversight is always to be exercised within and in relation to the whole Church. The Spirit who empowers those who are entrusted with oversight is the same Spirit who animates the life of all believers. On account of this, those who exercise oversight are inseparably bound to all believers. Those who exercise oversight have a special duty to care for, and recall the community to, the unity, holiness, catholicity and apostolicity of the Church. In discerning vocations and in ordaining others to share in the ministry of Word and Sacrament, they care for the continuity of the life of the Church. An important dimension of their oversight is care for the unity of the community, a unity which involves not only the mutual love of the members, but also their common confession of the apostolic faith, their nourishment by the Word and their life of common service in the world.

(II) COMMUNAL

96. One of the functions of episkopé is to care for the participation of the whole community in what makes for its common life and the discernment of the mind of the faithful. The communal life of the Church is grounded in the Sacrament of baptism. All the baptised share a

responsibility for the apostolic faith and witness of the whole Church. The communal dimension of the Church's life refers to the involvement of the whole body of the faithful in common consultation, sometimes through representation and constitutional structures, over the well-being of the Church and their common involvement in the service of God's mission in the world. Communal life sustains all the baptised in a web of belonging, of mutual accountability and support. It implies unity in diversity and is expressed in one heart and one mind (cf. Phil 2:1-2). It is the way in which Christians are held in unity and travel together as the one Church, and the one Church is manifested in the life of each local church.

(III) COLLEGIAL

97. Enabling the Church to live in conformity to the mission of Christ is a continuous process involving the whole community, but within that the gathering of those with oversight has a special role. Collegiality refers to the corporate, representative exercise in the areas of leadership, consultation, discernment, and decision-making. Collegiality entails the personal and relational nature of leadership and authority. Collegiality is at work wherever those entrusted with oversight gather, discern, speak and act as one on behalf of the whole Church. This implies leading the Church by means of the wisdom gained by corporate prayer, study and reflection, drawing on Scripture, tradition and reason – the wisdom and experience of all church communities throughout the ages. Sustaining collegiality involves preventing premature closure of debate, ensuring that different voices are heard, listening to expert opinion and drawing on appropriate sources of scholarship. Collegial oversight should help the Church to live in communion while the mind of Christ is being discerned. It makes room for those of different opinions, guarding and preaching unity, even call-

ing for restraint while giving spiritual and moral leadership. Speaking collegially can mean reflecting back to the community the legitimate diversity that exists within the life of the Church.

98. Because of the separation of the churches, there has been relatively little collegial exercise of oversight or witness within society on the part of the ministers of our divided communities. The ecumenical movement can serve as a stimulus and invitation to church leaders to explore the possibility of working together in appropriate ways on behalf of their own communities and as an expression of their care for all the churches (cf. 2 Cor 11:28), and in common witness before society.

G. Conciliarity and Primacy

99. Ministry and oversight, as treated in the previous two sections, are exercised locally and regionally. In addition, ecumenical dialogue has led the churches to ask whether and, if so, how they may function within the church as a communion existing throughout the whole world. Conciliarity and primacy concern the exercise of ministry at every level including this wider context. Conciliarity is an essential feature of the life of the Church, grounded in the common baptism of its members (cf. 1 Pet 2:9-10; Eph 4:11-16). Under the guidance of the Holy Spirit, the whole Church, whether dispersed or gathered together, is conciliar. Thus conciliarity characterises all levels of the life of the Church. It is already present in the relations which exist among the members of the smallest local communities; according to Gal 3:28, "you are all one in Christ Jesus", excluding divisions, domination, submission and all negative forms of discrimination. In the local Eucharistic community, conciliarity is the profound unity in love and truth between the members among themselves and with their presiding minister. This conciliar dimension is also expressed at

wider instances of Christian communion, some more regional and some even seeking to draw in the participation of the whole Christian community. The interconnectedness of the life of the Church is expressed between Christian communities at different geographic levels, the "all in each place" linked to the "all in every place".

100. In crucial situations synods came and come together to discern the apostolic truth over against particular threats and dangers to the life of the Church, trusting in the guidance of the Holy Spirit, whom Jesus promised to send after his return to the Father (cf. Jn 16:7.12-14; Acts 15:28). When synods drew together the leaders of the world Christian community, they were called "ecumenical", provided that their decrees were received by the whole Church. Their reception by the entire Church is an acknowledgement of the important service they have played in fostering and maintaining universal communion.

101. Wherever people, communities or churches come together to take counsel and make important decisions, there is need for someone to summon and preside over the gathering for the sake of good order and to help the process of promoting, discerning and articulating consensus. Those who preside are always to be at the service of those among whom they preside for the edification of the Church of God, in love and truth. It is the duty of the president to respect the integrity of local churches, to give voice to the voiceless and to uphold unity in diversity.

102. The word primacy was used by the Early Ecumenical Councils to refer to the ancient practice whereby the bishops of Alexandria, Rome and Antioch, and later Jerusalem and Constantinople, exercised a personal ministry of oversight over an area much wider than that of their individual ecclesiastical provinces. This suggests that primacy concerns the personal exercise of the ministry of oversight but also, since this exercise was

affirmed by the councils, that such oversight is not opposed to conciliarity, which expresses more the communal and collegial service to unity. Historically, forms of primacy have existed at various levels, some wider, such as those of the patriarchates, and some more restricted. According to canon 34 of the Apostolic Canons, the first among the bishops would only make a decision in agreement with the other bishops and the latter would make no important decision without the agreement of the first.

103. Even in the early centuries, primacy in the service of mission and unity became complicated by questions of jurisdiction and even competitiveness between patriarchates. The issues became more polarised as the papacy developed and further claims were made for the direct, immediate and universal jurisdiction of the Bishop of Rome over the whole Church. In recent years, however, both ecumenical rapprochement and globalisation have created a new climate in which a universal primacy can be seen as a gift rather than a threat to other churches and the distinctive features of their witness.

104. Partly because of the progress already recorded in bilateral and multilateral dialogues, the Fifth World Conference on Faith and Order raised the question "of a universal ministry of Christian unity". In his Encyclical *Ut Unum Sint*[20] Pope John Paul II quoted this text and invited church leaders and their theologians to "enter into patient and fraternal dialogue" concerning this ministry. This has led to an increasingly open debate. In subsequent discussion, despite continuing areas of disagreement, there seems to be an increasing openness to discuss a universal ministry in support of mission and unity of the church and agreement that any such personal ministry would need to be exercised in communal and collegial ways. Given the ecumenical sensitivity of this issue it is important to distinguish between the essence of the primacy and any particular ways in which it has been or is currently exercised.[21]

Conciliarity and Universal Primacy

There is still much work to be done to arrive at a preliminary convergence on this topic. At present Christians do not agree that universal ministry of conciliarity or primacy for the unity and mission of the church is necessary or acceptable. The lack of agreement is not simply between certain families of churches but exists within some churches. The way forward involves coming to a consensus both within each church and among the churches.

There has been significant ecumenical discussion of New Testament evidence about a ministry serving the wider unity of the Church, such as that of Peter or of Paul. Nevertheless, disagreements remain about the significance of their ministries and what they may imply for God's intention for some form of universal ministry in the service of the unity and mission of the Church.

H. Authority

105. Jesus' ministry was characterised with authority and healing which placed itself at the service of human beings. This authority was self-emptying with "power to lay down" his life (Jn 10:17-18). The vindication of this authority is eschatological (cf. 1 Cor. 15:28).

106. Authority is relational and interdependent. The ecclesiological theme of reception highlights the relation between authority and communion (cf. Jn 1:1-12). Christ's own exercise of authority is shown in his washing of his disciples' feet (cf. Jn 13:1-17). Mt 28:18-20 witnesses that Jesus gave his disciples the mandate to teach throughout the whole world and to relate their mission to the celebration of Christian initiation in baptism as well as to the faith in the Holy Trinity. In the opening scene of Acts

Jesus states that the power of the Holy Spirit will come upon the disciples and will give them authority to witness to the end of the world (Acts 1:7-8): "no one can say 'Jesus is Lord' except by the Holy Spirit" (1 Cor 12:3).

107. All authority in the church comes from God and is marked by God's holiness. This authority is effective when holiness shines from the lives of Christians and the ordered Christian community, faithful to the divine teachings. All the sources of authority recognised in varying degrees by the churches such as Scripture, tradition, worship, synods, also reflect the holiness of the Triune God.

108. One example of the communal aspect of authority in the church is the act of ordination. In ordination both the action of ordaining minister and the assent of the faithful are necessary elements.

IV. In and for the World

109. The reason for the mission of Jesus has been succinctly expressed in the words: "God so loved the world that he gave his only Son" (Jn 3:16). Thus the first and foremost attitude of God toward the world is love to every woman, man and child who has ever been born into human history.[22] The Kingdom of God, which Jesus preached in parables and inaugurated by his mighty deeds, especially by the paschal mystery of his death and resurrection, is the final destiny of the whole universe. One of the convictions which governs our reflections in this text is that the Church was intended by God, not for its own sake, but as an instrument, in God's hands, for the transformation of the world. Thus service (diakonia) belongs to the very being of the Church.[23]

110. One of the greatest services Christians offer to the world is the proclamation of the Gospel to every creature (cf. Mk.16:15). Evangelization is thus the foremost task of the church in obedience to the command of Jesus (Mt. 28:18-20). There is no contradiction between evangelisation and respect for the values present in other faiths.

111. The Church is the community of people called by God who, through the Holy Spirit, are united with Jesus Christ and sent as disciples to bear witness to God's reconciliation, healing and transformation of creation. Discipleship is based on the life and teaching of Jesus of Nazareth testified to in Scripture. Christians are called to respond to the living Word of God by obeying God rather than "any human truth" (Acts 5:29), by repenting of sinful actions, by forgiving others, and by living sacrificial lives of service. The source of their passion for the transformation of the world lies in their communion with God in Jesus Christ. They believe that God, who is absolute love, mercy and justice, is working through them by the Holy Spirit.

112. In the world which "God so loved" (John 3:16), Christians encounter not only situations of harmony and

prosperity, of progress and hope; but also problems and tragedies – sometimes of almost unspeakable magnitude – which demand from them a response as disciples of the One who healed the blind, the lame and the leper, who welcomed the poor and the outcast, and who challenged authorities who showed little regard for human dignity or the will of God. Precisely because of their faith, Christian communities may not stand idly by in the face of major calamities affecting human health, such as famine and starvation, natural disasters and the HIV/AIDS pandemic. Faith impels them to work for a more just social order, in which the goods of this earth, destined for the use of all, may be more justly shared, the suffering of the poor may be eased and absolute destitution may one day be eliminated. As followers of the One whom every Christmas they celebrate as the "Prince of Peace", Christians must advocate peace, especially by seeking to overcome the causes of war (principal among which are economic injustice, racism, ethnic and religious hatred, nationalism, and the use of violence to resolve differences and oppression). Jesus said that He came so that human beings may have life in abundance (cf. Jn 10:10); his followers must defend human life and dignity. Each context will provide its own clues to discern what is the appropriate Christian outreach in any particular circumstance. Even now, divided Christian communities can and sometimes have carried out this discernment together and have acted together to bring relief to suffering human beings and to help create a society more in keeping with their dignity and with the will of their loving Father in heaven.

113. The Christian community always lives within the sphere of divine forgiveness and grace. This grace calls forth and shapes the moral life of believers. Discipleship demands moral commitment. Members of the Church rely on God's forgiveness and renewing grace in all

moments of their lives, both in faithfulness and infidelity, either in virtue or in sin. The Church does not rest on moral achievement but on justification by grace through faith. It is of no little importance for the unity of the Church that the two communities whose separation marked the beginning of the Reformation have in recent years achieved consensus about the central aspects of the doctrine of justification by faith, the major doctrine at issue in their division.[24] It is on the basis of faith and grace that moral engagement and common action are possible and can even be affirmed as intrinsic to the life and being of the Church.

114. The ethics of Christians as disciples relate both to the Church and to the world.[25] They are rooted in God, the creator and revealer, and take shape as the community seeks to understand God's will within the various circumstances of time and place. The Church does not stand in isolation from the moral struggles of humankind as a whole. Christians both can and should join together with the adherents of other religions, as well as with all persons of good will, in order to promote not only those personal moral choices which they believe essential to the authentic realization of the human person, but also the social goods of justice, peace and the protection of the environment. Thus Christian discipleship requires believers to give serious consideration to the complex ethical questions that touch their personal lives and the public domain of social policy, and to translate their reflections into action. A Church that would want to be invisible would no longer be a church of disciples.

115. Not only must Christians seek to promote the values of the Kingdom of God by working together with adherents of other religions and even with those of no religious belief, but it is also incumbent upon them to witness to the Kingdom in the realms of politics and economics. In particular, despite dangers and distortions the

relation between Church and State has been, over the centuries, an arena for Christian advocacy for the transformation of society along the lines which Jesus sketched out in the Gospel. Many historical, cultural and demographic factors condition the relation between Church and State, or between Church and society.[26] One expression of the diversity or catholicity of the Church is the variety of models that these relations to societal structures can take. In each case, the explicit call of Jesus that his disciples be "salt of the earth" and "light of the world" (cf. Mt 5:13-16), and that they preach the Kingdom (the role of which in society is comparable to that of leaven which makes the whole dough rise (cf. Mt 13:33)), invites Christians to collaborate with political and economic authorities to promote the values of God's Kingdom, and to oppose policies and initiatives which contradict them. In this way Christians may stand in the tradition of the prophets who proclaimed God's judgement on all injustice.

116. There are occasions when ethical issues challenge the integrity of the Christian community itself and make it necessary to take a common stance to preserve its authenticity and credibility. Koinonia in relation to ethics and morals means that it is in the Church that, along with the confession of the faith and the celebration of the Sacraments (and as an inseparable part of these), the Gospel tradition is probed constantly for moral inspiration and insight. Situations where Christians or churches do not agree on an ethical position demand that dialogue continue in an effort to discover whether such differences can ultimately be overcome – and, if not, whether they are truly church-dividing.

117. Christians and their communities are called to be accountable to each other with respect to their ethical reflections and decisions. This interconnectedness is manifested in their commitment to the reciprocal partnership of giving and receiving (cf. Phil 4:15). As churches engage

in mutual questioning and affirmation, they give expression to what they share in Christ. Christians engage together in service to the world, glorifying and praising God and seeking that full koinonia, where the life which God desires for all people and the whole creation will find fulfilment.

118. "God did not send the Son into the world to condemn the world, but in order that the world might be saved through him" (Jn 3:17). The New Testament ends with the vision of a new heavens and a new earth, transformed by the grace of God (cf. Rev 21:1-22:5). This new world is promised for the end of history, but even now the Church, on a pilgrimage of faith and hope marching through time, calls out in worship "Come, Lord Jesus" (Rev 22:20). Christ loves the Church as the bridegroom loves his bride (cf. Eph 5:25) and, until the wedding feast of the lamb in the Kingdom of heaven (cf. Rev 19:7), shares with it his mission of bringing light and healing to human beings until he comes again in glory.

Conclusion

119. In recent years the ecumenical movement has produced many agreed statements recording converging understandings about the faith and order of the Church. Among the most well known of these is Baptism, Eucharist and Ministry. Such converging understandings have challenged some churches to accept into their life the implications of their common affirmations. Significant proposals for steps towards greater expressions of visible unity have been enacted, or are awaiting decision, by the churches in virtually every part of the world. This ecumenical fact deserves affirmation.

120. Progress has shown itself concretely in the ways by which churches, according to various criteria and to varying degrees, have engaged in processes of reception and thus have advanced towards mutual recognition - or at least towards the recognition of Christian faith and life beyond their preconceived boundaries, as they formally understand them to be. Some have reached a stage of mutual recognition.

121. However, this convergence has not been received everywhere. There has been a significant retrenchment in some areas, expressed in a re-confessionalism or an anti-ecumenical spirit. There are also examples of non-reception which are either the result of deeply held theological convictions, or of the shortcomings of the ecumenical work itself. All the churches, at all levels of their life, are called upon to engage in the task of articulating together a common understanding of Christian identity: the dynamic and pilgrim character of the people of God, constantly called to repentance and renewal.

122. Ultimately the reception of the results of theological convergence will lead us to what the Canberra Statement called for: "The goal of the search for full communion is realised when all the churches are able to recognise in one another the one, holy, catholic and apostolic church in its fullness" and express this in a reconciled common life.

123. Building on the convergence of earlier work, this present document is an attempt to express what the churches might now claim together about the nature and mission of the Church; and, within that perspective, to state the remaining areas of difficulty and disagreement. If the churches were able to agree together to a convergence statement on the Church, this would further significantly the process of mutual recognition on the way to reconciliation and visible unity.

NOTES

1 "Faith and Order By-Laws, 3.1", in *Faith and Order at the Crossroads: The Plenary Commission Meeting, Kuala Lumpur 2004*, Thomas F. Best ed., Faith and Order Paper no. 196, Geneva, WCC, 2005, p.450.

2 *The Ecumenical Movement: An Anthology of Key Texts and Voices*, Michael Kinnamon and Brian E. Cope eds, Geneva and Grand Rapids, WCC and Eerdmans, 1997, pp.124-25.

3 *Towards a Common Understanding and Vision of the World Council of Churches: A Policy Statement*, Geneva, WCC, Sept. 1997.

4 Faith and Order Paper no. 111, Geneva, WCC, 1982.

5 Faith and Order Paper no. 153, new rev. version, 4th printing, Geneva, WCC, 1996.

6 Faith and Order Paper no. 151, 2nd rev. printing, Geneva, WCC, 1990.

7 Faith and Order Paper no. 181, Geneva, WCC, 1998.

8 Cf. "Towards a Common Understanding of the Church: Reformed-Roman Catholic Dialogue", §96, in *Growth in Agreement II: Reports and Agreed Statements of Ecumenical Conversations on a World Level, 1982-1998*, Faith and Order Paper no. 187, ed. by Jeffrey Gros, Harding Meyer, William G. Rusch, Geneva and Grand Rapids, WCC and Eerdmans, 2000, p.802.

9   *Confessing the One Faith*, §240.

10 Cf. Report of Section II: "Multiplicity of Expression of the One Faith", §§13-22, in *On the Way to Fuller Koinonia: Official Report of the Fifth World Conference on Faith and Order*, ed. by Thomas F. Best and Günther Gassman, Faith and Order Paper no. 161, Geneva, WCC, pp. 240-242.

11 Cf. §12 of the present study document.

12 Cf. *A Treasure in Earthen Vessels: An Instrument for an Ecumenical Reflection on Hermeneutics*, Faith and Order Paper no. 182, Geneva, WCC, 1998, §§49ff., and the draft text from the Faith and Order study on *Ethnic Identity, National Identity and the Search for the Unity of the Church*: "Participation in God's Mission of Reconciliation: An Invitation to the Churches", FO/2005:11, June 2005, Section II. (To be published in revised form as a Faith and Order Paper).

13 *A Treasure in Earthen Vessels*, §38.

14 See *Confessing the One Faith*.

15 *A Treasure in Earthen Vessels*, Section B, 1. (§§38-42).

16 Cf. §12 of the present study document.

17 "Baptism" section, in *Baptism, Eucharist and Ministry*, §9.

18 Cf. the text-in-process from the Faith and Order study on Baptism: "One Baptism: Towards Mutual Recognition", FO/2005:06, June 2005, §35.

19 It is hoped that the Faith and Order study on Baptism presently underway will help to resolve these outstanding problems. Cf. the text-in-process from the Faith and Order study on Baptism: "One Baptism: Towards Mutual Recognition", FO/2005:06, June 2005.

20 John Paul II, *Ut Unum Sint: Encyclical Letter of the Holy Father John Paul II on Commitment to Ecumenism*, London, Catholic Truth Society, 1995, §96.

21 Any "universal ministry of Christian unity" needs to be exercised in a communal and collegial way, resembling Faith and Order's perspective on ministry as expressed in Baptism, Eucharist and Ministry, "Ministry" Section, §26.

22 Cf. the study document from the Faith and Order study on theological anthropology: "Ecumenical Perspectives on Theological Anthropology", Faith and Order Paper no. 199, Geneva, WCC, 2005, Section II.
23 Cf. *Church and World*, passim.
24 See *Joint Declaration on the Doctrine of Justification, The Lutheran World Federation and the Roman Catholic Church*, English language edition, Grand Rapids, Michigan and Cambridge, U.K., William B. Eerdmans, 2000; available online at: http://www.elca.org/ ecumenical/ecumenicaldialogue/romancatholic/jddj/declaration.html.
25 Cf. the text-in-process from the Faith and Order study on Baptism: "One Baptism: Towards Mutual Recognition", §58, §77.
26 Cf. the draft text from the Faith and Order study on *Ethnic Identity, National Identity and the Search for the Unity of the Church*: "Participation in God's Mission of Reconciliation: An Invitation to the Churches", Section IV, A.

IMPRIMERIE
LUSSAUD
OFFSET&NUMERIQUE

L'impression et le façonnage
de cet ouvrage
ont été effectués
à l'Imprimerie LUSSAUD
85200 Fontenay-le-Comte

Dépôt légal 4ᵉ trimestre 2005
n° 4008
N° d'impression : 204 339